It depends.
状況によります。
（ケースバイケースです。）

That makes sense.
理にかなってる。（それはそうだね。）

Keep your chin up!
元気出して！がんばってね。

Go ahead.
お先にどうぞ。

It's up to you.
きみ次第だよ。

I'll be bac
すぐに戻りま

I'm in a hurry.
急...

I'll be right there.
すぐに行きます。

I feel much better.
だいぶ気分が良くなりました。

The sooner, the better.
早ければ早いほど良い。

How was it?
どうだった？

It was fun.
おもしろかった。

I got it.
了解！

I changed my mind.
気が変わりました。

It was nice meeting you.
お会いできてよかった。

Let's get going.
さあ行こう。

For here or to go?
ここで食べる？持ち帰る？

Are you ready to go?
もう出発できる？

Third-person singular
三単現 s

Prepositions
前置詞

Adverbs
副詞

Future tense
未来形

Comparatives
比較級

Past tense be verbs
Be 動詞の過去

Past tense
一般動詞の過去

Gerunds
動名詞

Infinitives
不定詞

CONTENTS

Learning World 4
STUDENT BOOK
BRIDGE

with **Mikiko Nakamoto**

JJ

Daisuke

Ann

Eve

Lisa

本書は、使える英語を目的とした幼児・児童英語教育を3〜5年ほど学習した児童が中学英語にスムーズに進むことを目的に編集されています。「言語を使うこと」に焦点を置き、既習の英語表現の規則を整理することによって、より複雑な英文を読んだり、より深い自己表現ができるよう構成されています。

　本書の各STEPは動物の写真を使ったAnimal Talk、Learning World Book 3までの文型を使ったコミュニケーション活動（Let's get started using...）、文法の定着のためのチャンツ（Let's Chant!）、ターゲットの文法説明（Let's Study）、ターゲットの構文を使ったオーセンティックなWriting（Let's Write）、ターゲットの構文を使って課題を解き、その結果をクラスの前で発表するLet's Plan and Make a Presentation、リスニングテスト（Let's Listen）の7つのセクションで構成されています。

　本書では英文をできる限り自然でオーセンティックにするためLearning World Book 3までの語彙や句がランダムに出てきますが、各STEPの文法説明は中学英語の学習順に沿って編集しています。中学英語の導入期の副教材として「英語を使う」ことを目的として使用することも可能です。

Animal Talk

動物達のユーモアあふれる会話を通して英語で共感。動物になりきって言ってみましょう。

Let's get started using ...

「文法」は後回し、まず英語を使って課題を解決しましょう。

Let's Chant!

「まず使ってみた英語」の構文は場面のあるチャンツで定着。

Let's Study

文構造を「使う」ことを目的にわかりやすく解説。読んで納得！

One more chant!

構文はリズムをつけて丸ごと暗記。

Let's Write

ターゲットの構文を使って、「実際のこと」を英文で書いてみましょう。

Let's Plan and Make a Presentation

ターゲットの構文を使って、個人やグループの考えをまとめて発表しましょう。

Let's Listen

自然な会話の中からポイントとなる情報を聞き取るリスニング問題に挑戦。

Achievement Targets これだけできるようにがんばろう。

STEPs 1-6

1 テキストの (チャンツ)のうち4つのチャンツを大きな声で暗唱できます。
Able to recite four 'Let's Chants' in a loud, clear voice.　⑤ ⑨ ⑬ ⑰ ㉑ ㉕

2 テキストの **Animal Talk** を4つ、友達と感情をこめて言うことができます。
Able to say four 'Animal Talk' dialogues with a partner.　④ ⑧ ⑫ ⑯ ⑳ ㉔

3 テキストの **One more chant!** の11個のうち7つを大きな声で暗唱できます。⑥ ⑩ ⑩ ⑭ ⑭ ⑱ ⑱ ㉒ ㉒ ㉖ ㉖
Able to recite seven 'One more chants' in a loud, clear voice.

4 **Let's Write** のコーナーを1つ選び、自分の答えを暗唱し発表することができます。⑦ ⑪ ⑮ ⑲ ㉓ ㉗
Able to remember and present my answers for one 'Let's Write'.

5 I am を使って自分のことが5つ言えます。
Able to say five things about myself using, "I am…"

6 Will you …? を使って先生に3つお願いができます。
Able to make three requests to my teacher, using, "Will you …?"

7 Do you …? を使って先生に質問が8つできます。
Able to ask eight questions to my teacher, using "Do you…?"

8 各STEPの Mini Test を80%正解しました。
Able to get more than 80% on each 'Mini Test'.

STEPs 7-12

9 テキストの (チャンツ)のうち4つのチャンツを大きな声で暗唱できます。
Able to recite four 'Let's Chants' in a loud, clear voice.　㉙ ㉝ ㉗ ㊶ ㊺ ㊾

10 テキストの **Animal Talk** を4つ、友達と感情をこめて言うことができます。
Able to say four 'Animal Talk' dialogues with a partner.　㉘ ㉜ ㊱ ㊵ ㊹ ㊽

11 テキストの **One more chant!** の6個のうち4つを大きな声で暗唱できます。
Able to recite four 'One more chants' in a loud, clear voice.　㉚ ㉞ ㊳ ㊷ ㊻ ㊿

12 **Let's Write** のコーナーを1つ選び、自分の答えを暗唱し発表することができます。
Able to remember and present my answers for one 'Let's Write'.　㉛ ㉟ ㊴ ㊸ ㊼ 51

13 友達を1人選び、その人を10以上の文章を使って紹介することができます。
Able to introduce a friend, using at least ten sentences.

14 自分の得意なことを8つ以上の文章を使って言うことができます。
Able to tell what you are good at, using at least eight sentences.

15 There is/are, on, in, under, by などを使って教室内にあるものを5個言うことができます。
Able to tell the location of five objects in the room using, "There is/are", "on", "in", "under", "by", etc.

16 各STEPの Mini Test を80%正解しました。
Able to get more than 80% on each 'Mini Test'.

STEPs 13-18

17 テキストの (チャンツ)のうち4つのチャンツを大きな声で暗唱できます。
Able to recite four 'Let's Chants' confidently in a loud, clear voice.　53 57 61 65 69 73

18 テキストの **Animal Talk** を4つ、友達と感情をこめて言うことができます。
Able to say four 'Animal Talk' dialogues with a partner.　52 56 60 64 68 72

19 テキストの **One more chant!** の9個のうち6つを大きな声で暗唱できます。54 54 58 62 66 66 70 70 74
Able to recite six 'One more chants' in a loud, clear voice.

20 **Let's Write** のコーナーを1つ選び、自分の答えを暗唱し発表することができます。55 59 63 67 71 75
Able to remember and present my answers for one 'Let's Write'.

21 2つの物を比べて発表できます。
Able to present the differences and similarities between two items.

22 昨日したことを10個言うことができます。
Able to tell ten things about what I did yesterday.

23 I know a man (woman) who can (is,was) を使って自分の知っている人を紹介できます。
Able to introduce someone using, "I know a man/woman who can/is/was…"

24 各STEPの Mini Test を80%正解しました。
Able to get more than 80% on each 'Mini Test'.

○の中の数字はページをあらわしています。

自分のことを言ってみよう！

Animal Talk

3

I am a rabbit.
I am not a cat.

ぼくはうさぎ。
ねこではありません。

I know. わかってるよ。
I am a cat.
I am not a rabbit.

私はねこ。うさぎじゃないよ。

I am a dog.　I am a panda.

まず、使ってみよう！
Let's get started using "I am ..."

I am, you are, we are, they are,

　　　　　he is, she is, it is, too.

I am happy, you are happy,

　　　　we are happy, they are happy.

He is happy, she is happy,

　　　　it is happy, too.　**GREAT!**

JJ　　　Daisuke　　Ann　　Eve　　Lisa

■「～です」と言いたい時は英語では **Be** ファミリーを使います。

「～です」や「～にいます」には **am** と **is** と **are** があります。

みんな **Be** ファミリーの一員です。

I の時は私にお任せくださ〜い。

1 「**私は〜です**」を練習しましょう。

I **am** Lisa.

I **am** a student.

I **am** happy.

I **am** from Japan.

「です」の私が、ここにいるので〜す。

私は　です　リサ

2 主語（だれのことを言うか）によって **Be** ファミリーの他のメンバー **are, is** を使います。

You
We
They
are

You are　　We are　　They are
「あなたは〜です。　私たちは〜です。　彼らは〜です。」の時はぼくの出番です。

He
She
It
is

He is　　She is　　It is　　Mr. Be is
「彼は〜です。　彼女は〜です。　それは〜です。　Beさんは〜です。」の時は私の出番です。

3 「**〜ではありません**」と言う時

否定する時は、ぼくがここに入るんだ。

短く言うこともできるよ。

私は　です　ではない　リサ

I am = I'm　**are not = aren't**　**is not = isn't**

I **am not** Lisa.　　　= I'**m not** Lisa.

You **are not** Lisa. = You **aren't** Lisa.

She **is not** Lisa.　= She **isn't** Lisa.

It **is not** a cat.　　= It **isn't** a cat.

4 「**〜ですか？**」と質問する時

質問する時は、こう並ぶんだもん！

書く時は、最初を大文字にするのを忘れないで！

です　私は　リサ

Am I Lisa?　　　Yes, you are.　　No, you are not.

Are you Lisa?　　Yes, I am.　　　No, I am not.

Is she Lisa?　　　Yes, she is.　　No, she is not.

Is it a cat?　　　Yes, it is.　　　No, it is not.

🔵 **One more chant!**

6

I'm sleepy,　Are you sleepy?　No, I'm not.　I'm not sleepy yet.

He's sleepy,　Is he sleepy?　No, he's not.　He's not sleepy yet.

She's sleepy,　Is she sleepy?　No, she's not.　She's not sleepy yet.

He is = He's　　**She is = She's**

5 「**〜にいます**」「**〜にあります**」と言う時も **am, is, are** を使います。

I **am** (I'm) here.　　　　　　　　　　　私はここにいます。

My school **is** in front of the station.　　　私の学校は駅の前にあります。

Write each sentence. If they are not true for you, rewrite them using "not".
次の文章を必要があれば否定して、必要がなければそのまま書きましょう。

1 I am a student.

2 I am always happy.

3 I am from Hokkaido.

4 I am thirteen years old.

5 I am a good listener.

6 I am good at sports.

7 I am punctual.

Let's Plan and Make a Presentation

Me & My Friend   Introduce yourself and a friend.
自分のことと友達のことを紹介しましょう。

Hello, everyone.

● My name is _____. Please call me _____.

● I am _____ . I _____ years old.

● I am good at _____.

● _____ is my friend. He/She is _____ years old.

● He/She _____ and _____.

● I'm very happy to be here with my friend _____ today.
  Thank you.

Let's Listen

p.4 の絵を見ながら答えましょう。

1 _____   **2** _____   **3** _____   **4** _____

Animal Talk

What is that? あれ何？
Is it a panda? パンダ？

Hi...

No way! It is not a panda.
ばっかじゃないの。パンダじゃないよ。
It is a dog. 犬でしょ。

まず、使ってみよう！

Let's get started using "Is it ...?"

8→9

What's this?　　　What's this?　　　What is this?

It's a book.　　　It's a book.　　　It's **my** book.

What's that?　　　What's that?　　　What is that?

It's a bag.　　　It's a bag.　　　It's **your** bag.

What's this?　　　What's this?　　　What is this?

It's an eraser.　　　It's an eraser.　　　It's **his** eraser.

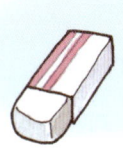

What's that?　　　What's that?　　　What is that?

It's a stapler.　　　It's a stapler.　　　It's **her** stapler.

That's our school!

■「～は何ですか？」とたずねる時は **What** で始め、質問する時の順でたずねます。

何かわからない時は、まず **What**！　　質問する時の順番で並びます。　　書く時はこれを忘れずに！

1 **What** の後は質問する時の順でたずねます。 答えには **It is ...** を使います。

What?	何？（聞き返す時）
What is this?	これは　何ですか。 It is a stapler.
What is that?	あれは　何ですか。 It is a staple.

What is = What's　　It is = It's

2 **What** を使っていろいろなことを質問することができます。

何か	What is a UFO?	It is an unidentified flying object.
名前	What is your name?	My name is Sakura.
時刻	What time is it?	It is eight o'clock.
曜日	What day is it today?	It is Monday.
日付	What is the date today?	It is May seventh.

3 「**This is ...** これは〜です。 **That is ...** あれは〜です。」の使い方を練習しましょう。

This is a frog. It is not a ball.

That is a ball. It is not a frog.

決まった言い方を丸ごと覚えましょう。

This is my friend.	こちらは私の友達です。
This is Lisa speaking.	（電話で）リサです。
Who is it?	（ドアのノックの音を聞いて）どなたですか？

4 「私の〜」と言う時は **I** ではなく **my** を使います。

ぼくは「ぼくの」に変わらなきゃいけないんだ。

- you は **your** に変わるんだ。
- he は **his** 、she は **her** になります。
- we は **our** 、they は **their** 、it は **its** になります。
- 人の名前（**Tom**）は **Tom's** に変わるんだ。

🔘 **One more chant!**

10 My house, your house, his house, her house, our house, their house, Mr. Miller's house! My car, your car, his car, her car, our car, their car, Mr. Miller's car!

5 「**だれですか?**」と質問する時は **Who** を最初に言います。

🔘 **One more chant!**

11 Who's she? She is my mother. What's her name? Her name is Nancy. Who's he? He is my father. What's his name? His name is Paul.

Who's = Who is

Let's Write

Complete the sentences using "is" or "isn't" in 1-4. Write the answers in 5-7.
1-4は is または isn't を入れて英文を完成させましょう。5-7は質問に答えましょう。

1 A whale _____ an animal.

2 A puppy _____ a baby cat.

3 The capital city of the USA _____ New York.

4 The sun _____ a star, but the earth _____ a star.

5 What time is it? _____

6 What day is it today? _____

7 What is the date today? _____

Let's Plan and Make a Presentation

Japanese Items   Choose an item and describe it.

Task   下の写真の中から１つ選び説明しましょう。

My Idea

This is _____.

It is _____.

Group Summary

This is _____.

It is _____.

Let's Listen

p.8の1~13の絵を見ながら答えましょう。

1 ⬭   **2** ⬭   **3** ⬭   **4** ⬭

Animal Talk

I like you.
きみのこと、だいすき。

Let's play!
あそぼうよ。

Don't hug me!
ハグしないで！

まず、使ってみよう！

Let's get started using "wash, wash the dishes"

wash	give	set	eat	watch
read	drive	buy	feed	sing
open	write	drink	draw	speak
play	study	cook	practice	ride
close	answer	take	bake	make

13→14

 Sing!

Sing a song.

Let's sing a song.

"Shall I sing a song?" or "Will you sing a song?"

Or "Shall we sing a song?"

Sh.... Don't sing a song!

Sh...

■ 「動作を表す」言葉には、「実際に動作が見える」言葉と、
「行為が続いている状態を表す」言葉があります。

walk

want

1 動作を表す言葉を練習しましょう。

● 「歩く、泳ぐ、走る」のように、実際に見える動作を表す言葉

climb cook cry drink drive eat fly jump laugh look move open play
pull push read say sit skate ski sleep speak stand study swim write

One more chant!

15

Go. Let's go. Run. Let's run. Walk. Let's walk. Sing. Let's sing.
Dance. Let's dance. Shout. Let's shout. Stop. Let's stop!

● 「〜を好き、〜をほしい、〜を知っている、住んでいる、〜を持っている」のように、
見えないけれど行為が続いている状態を表す言葉

like   want   know   live   have   love   need

2 「何を」するのかを入れて練習しましょう。

drive	drive a car	want	want a dog
open	open the window	like	like English
play	play soccer	have	have a sister
study	study math	know	know the results
write	write a letter	need	need a dictionary

3 人に**命令する時**は、動作を表す言葉で始めます。ていねいに言う時には **please** を付けます。

▌**Speak** English in the classroom.   ▌**Speak English, please.**

4 「**一緒にしよう**」と誘う時は **Let's** を先に言います。

▌**Let's** speak English in the classroom.   ▌**Let's** sing a song.   ▌**Let's** play soccer.

5 「**してはいけない**」と命令する時は **Don't** を先に言います。

▌**Don't** watch TV.   ▌**Don't** read comics.   ▌**Don't** make noise.

Go out.   **Don't** go out.   **Let's** go out.

6 「**私が〜しましょうか？**」は **Shall I** 、「**〜していただけますか？**」は **Will you** 、
「**一緒に〜しませんか？**」は **Shall we** を最初に言います。

 One more chant!

16

Shall I drive a car?   Will you drive a car?   Shall we drive a car? ××××
Shall I open the window? Will you open the window? Shall we open the window? ××××

■ Write all the actions the animals do.

1 dogs

2 lions

3 snakes

4 bears

5 birds

6 monkeys

7 kangaroos

8 frogs

9 fish

10 whales

11 humans

> bark   dig   fly   grab things   jump   roar   run   swim   talk   walk
> shed their skin   breathe in water   climb a tree   feed babies their milk

Let's Plan and Make a Presentation

Animals   Choose an animal and describe its life and environment.
動物を1つ選び、その生態についてスピーチしましょう。

Task

1 Let me talk about _____.

2 They live _____.

> in the ocean   in fields   in the sky   in jungles   in Africa
> in rivers   in ponds   on land   at the South Pole

3 They _____.

> swim   walk   run   fly   jump

Draw the animal.

4 They eat _____.

5 They have _____.

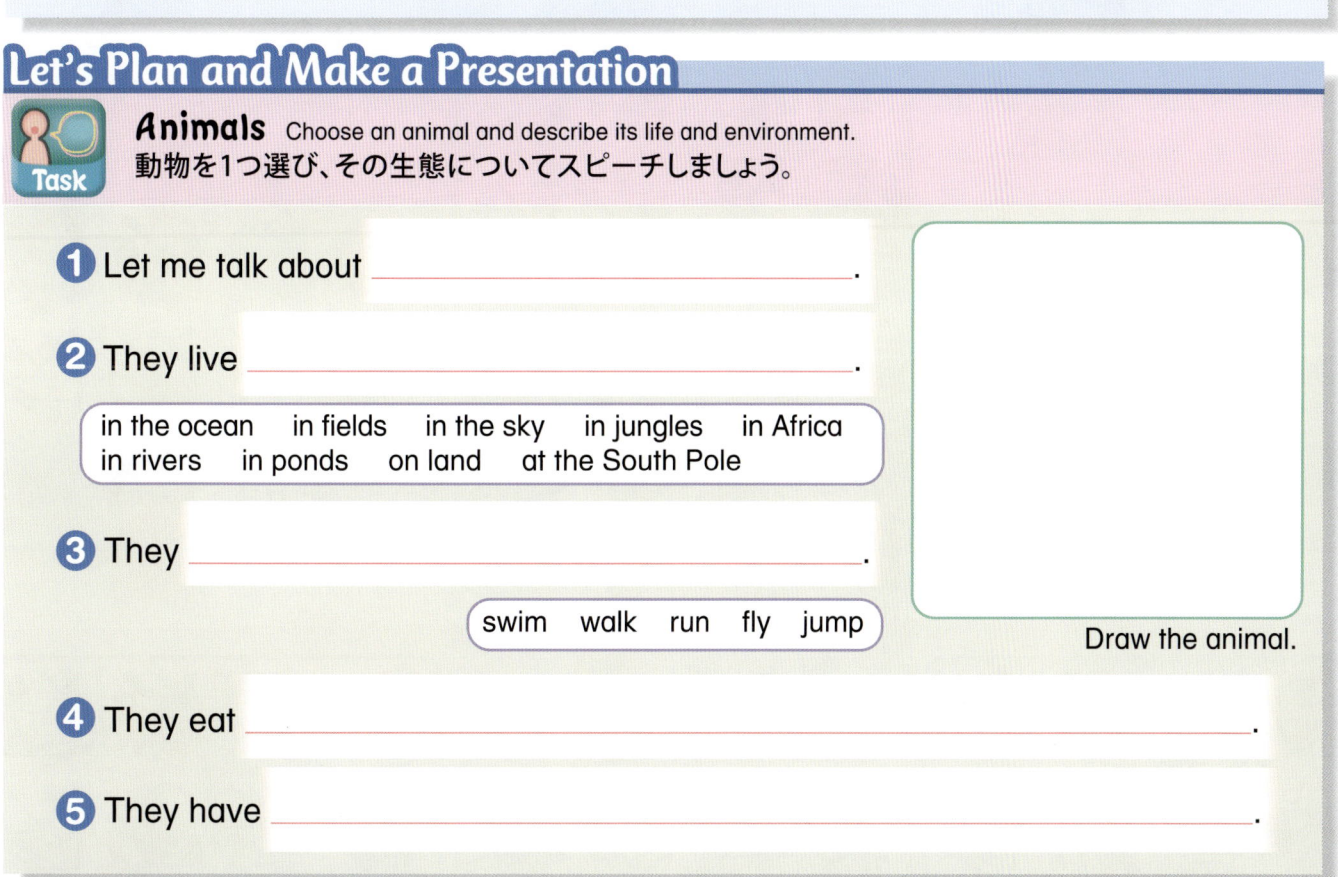

Let's Listen

1	**2**	**3**	**4**
a. by car	**a.** pop	**a.** piano	**a.** winter
b. walk	**b.** hot chocolate	**b.** sing	**b.** skiing
c. run	**c.** water	**c.** guitar	**c.** swimming

Animal Talk

17

Mom, do you like milk?
ママ、ミルク好き？

No, I don't.
いいえ。

Drink it up.
飲んでしまいなさい。

まず、使ってみよう！
Let's get started using "Do you like ...?"

JJ

Ann

Lisa

Yumi

Daisuke

Eve

Min

Ema

Mark

Nelson

18→19

Do you like dogs?

Yes, I do. Yes, I do. I like dogs.

Do you like snakes?

No, I don't. No, I don't. I don't like snakes.

Do you like cats?

Yes, I do. Yes, I do.

I like cats.

Do you like spiders?

No, I don't. No, I don't.

I don't like spiders.

■「私は〜」と言う時は、一番最初に **I** 、その次に動作を表す言葉を言います。

まず私！　犬が好き！

1 「自分」のことを言う時は **I** を最初に言います。

One more chant!
20

drive   drive a car   I drive a car.   want   want a dog   I want a dog.
open   open the window   I open the window. like   like English   I like English.
play   play soccer   I play soccer.   have   have a sister   I have a sister.

2 「相手」のことは **You**、「自分たち」のことを言う時は **We** を最初に言います。

❚ **I** want a dog.   ❚ **You** want a dog.   ❚ **We** want a dog.

3 「〜ではない」と言う時は **I** の後に **do not (= don't)** を言います。

ねえ、ぼくも入れてー

えー!!　**don't** が入っちゃうの!?

don't が入ると
「〜ではない」という
意味になります。

私は　　〜ではない　　犬をほしい

❚ **I don't** want a dog.

4 相手に質問する時は **Do you** で始めます。（書く時は最初の文字を大文字にして、最後には？を付けましょう）

質問の時は、まずぼくがくる。

 Yes, I do.

 No, I don't.

〜ですか　　あなたは　　犬をほしい

❚ **Do you** want a dog**?**

｜ Yes, I do.   I want a dog.
No, I don't. I don't want a dog.

One more chant!
21

want   want a dog   I want a dog.   Do you want a dog? Yes, I do.
drive   drive a car   I drive a car.   Do you drive a car? No, I don't.

5 2つ以上の言葉が集まって1つの動作を表す言葉もあります。

get up	Time to get up.	put on	Put on your jacket.
get on	Get on the train.	take off	Take off your shoes.
get off	Get off the bus.	give up	Don't give up.
turn on	Turn on the TV.	hand in	Hand in the paper.
turn off	Turn off the light.	run away	Don't run away.

Let's Write

■ Write each sentence. If they are not true for you, rewrite them using "not".

1 I speak Japanese. _____

2 I need a new dictionary. _____

3 I speak Chinese. _____

4 I like science. _____

5 I wear glasses. _____

6 I brush my teeth three times a day.

_____

Let's Plan and Make a Presentation

 **Task**

Cats or Dogs? Are you a dog person or a cat person? Conduct a survey and explain the results.
あなたは犬派？ それとも猫派？ クラス調査をし、結果を発表しましょう。

Do you (like **have** **want**) dogs or cats?   ¹| ²|| ³||| ⁴|||| ⁵||||

	both dogs and cats	dogs	cats	neither dogs nor cats	TOTAL
1 like					
2 have					
3 want					

We conducted a survey of _____ **people. As a result,**

_____ people (like have want) dogs.

_____ people (like have want) cats.

_____ people (like have want) both dogs and cats.

_____ people (like have want) neither dogs nor cats.

Let's Listen

p.16の絵（Min, Mark, Nelsonを除く）を見ながら答えましょう。

 JJ    Ann    Lisa    Daisuke    Yumi    Eve    Ema

( )   ( )   ( )   ( )   ( )   ( )   ( )

Animal Talk

♪ 22

> **How many children do you have?**
> 子供、何羽いるの？

> **Let me see.** ちょっと待ってね。
> **One, two, three, four...**
> 1, 2, 3, 4 …
>
> **Four... I think.** たぶん4羽。

まず、使ってみよう！
Let's get started using "How many ...?"

1
2
3
4
5
6
7
8
9
10

Let's Chant!

A dog. Look! More than one. Dogs.

A cat. Look! More than one. Cats.

A pig. Look! More than one. Pigs.

A goose. Look! More than one. Geese.

A mouse. Look! More than one. Mice.

A sheep. Look! More than one. Well … Sheep!

■「1つ」「2つ以上」「ない＝ゼロ」の時、英語では言い方が変わります。

an apple	apples	no apples
a carrot	carrots	no carrots
a peach	peaches	no peaches

1つの物を表す時は、言葉の前に a か an を付けます。
2つ以上の物には言葉の最後に s か es が付きます。言葉によって s や es の音が変化します。

1 数えられる物が２つ以上の時は、最後に **s** か **es** を付けます。その他いろいろな形を練習しましょう。

a book ⟶ book**s**	a cap ⟶ cap**s**	a desk ⟶ desk**s**
an orange ⟶ orange**s**	a pencil ⟶ pencil**s**	a teacher ⟶ teacher**s**
a baby ⟶ bab**ies**	a story ⟶ stor**ies**	a city ⟶ cit**ies**
a bus ⟶ bus**es**	a dish ⟶ dish**es**	a class ⟶ class**es**
a knife ⟶ kni**ves**	a leaf ⟶ lea**ves**	a life ⟶ li**ves**
a goose ⟶ **geese**	a mouse ⟶ **mice**	a child ⟶ **children**
a sheep ⟶ **sheep**	a fish ⟶ **fish**	a Japanese ⟶ **Japanese**
this ⟶ **these**	that ⟶ **those**	

ヘッ！
ぼくたちはずっと
同じだもん

sheep sheep

私たち、数えられないものは変わりませ～ん！

water　air　love　money　music

 **One more chant!**

25

What're these? What're these? What are these?
　They are markers. They are markers. They are my markers.
What're those? What're those? What are those?
　They are rulers. They are rulers. They are my rulers.

what are = what're

2 数を聞く時は **How many ...s** で始めます。

How many?

How many coins?

How many coins do you have?

　　　　I have some coins.　I have three coins.

　　　　I don't have any coins.　I have no coins!

 One more chant!

26

How many boys? Let me count.　One, two, three! Three boys!
How many girls? Let me count. One, two, three, four, five, six, seven. Seven girls!

3 数えられないものの量を聞く時は **How much** で始めます。

How much?

How much money?

How much money do you have?

　　　　I have some money.

　　　　I don't have any money.

　　　　I have no money.

Do you have any money with you?
お金の持ち合わせある？

I have no money with me.

Complete the sentences using the key words.

1 sister   I have _____ .

2 brother   I have _____ .

3 eraser   I have _____ at home.

4 bicycle   In my family, we have _____ .

5 player   We need _____ for soccer / rugby.

6 class   I have _____ today.

7 national holiday   We have _____ in a year.

Let's Plan and Make a Presentation

Task

Let's Make Lunch   You are going to make lunch for 10 friends. Decide what to make, and make your shopping list.
10人の友達を呼んでランチパーティーをすることになりました。何を作るか考えてショッピングリストを作りましょう。

My Idea   I want to make _____ .

Group Summary

We are going to make _____ and _____ .

Shopping List

what we need	how much / how many	what we need	how much / how many

Let's Listen

p.20の1~6の絵を見ながら答えましょう。

1 (____)   **2** (____)   **3** (____)   **4** (____)

Animal Talk

27

Yoo-hoo! やっほ～！
I am here at the top
of the tree.
木のてっぺんにいるよ。

What? えっ！
Where? どこって？
Why? なぜ？
How? どうやって？

まず、使ってみよう！
Let's get started using "Where, When, How"

Ann: Let's go to the museum on Saturday by bike.

Daisuke: Let's go to the park on Sunday by bike.

Eve: Let's go to the park on Sunday by car.

Lisa: Let's go to the park on Sunday by bus.

JJ: Let's go to the park on Saturday by car.

Mark: Let's go to the park on Saturday by bus.

Yumi: Let's go to the museum on Sunday by car.

Min: Let's go to the park on Saturday by bike.

Nelson: Let's go to the museum on Sunday by bike.

Ema: Let's go to the museum on Saturday by car.

 Sat
 Sun

Let's Chant!

28→29

Where, where, where?

Where shall we go?

To the park, to the park.

Let's go to the park.

When, when, when?

When shall we go?

On Sunday, on Sunday.

Let's go on Sunday.

How, how, how?

How shall we go?

By bike, by bike.

Let's go by bike.

That sounds great!

■ いろいろなことを質問する時は、一番聞きたいことを最初に言います。

たいていのわからないことは
ぼくたち Wh 隊で解決します！

ぼくも Wh 隊の仲間です！

What なに？

Where どこ？

Who だれ？

When いつ？

Why なぜ？

How どのように？

1 「何か」「どこに」「いつ」「なぜ」「だれ」「どのように」を練習しましょう。

30 **One more chant!**

What is it? Where is it? When is it? Why is it? Who is it? How is it?

2 「何か」がわからない時はまず **What**、その後、質問文の順でたずねます。

▎ **What** ＋ do you have?

わからない時は質問の形でぼくの後についてきてくださ ーい！

何を きみはほしいの？	**What** do you want?
どこに きみは行くの？	**Where** do you go?
いつ きみは行くの？	**When** do you go?
なぜ きみは行くの？	**Why** do you go?
どのように きみは行くの？	**How** do you go?

日本語の順番をちょっと
変えるとわかりやすいよ！

31 **One more chant!**

Where do you go? When do you go? How do you go? Why do you go?
And what do you want to do there?

3 くわしく聞きたい時は **What, Whose, Which** のすぐ後に、質問したいものを続けて言います。

What sport do you play?
What time do you get up?
What kind of music do you like?

Whose bag is this?
Which ice cream do you want?
Which month is the coldest?

きみたち、だ〜れ？

Who are you?

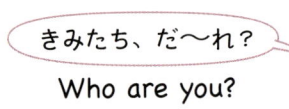

ぼくたちも仲間に入れて〜！

4 **How** は、いろいろなものの「どのくらい」に使うこともできます。

How old is your grandmother?
How many brothers do you have?
How tall are you?
How much is it?
How often do you brush your teeth?

■ Write about yourself.

1 Where do you live? _____

2 How do you spell your last name? _____

3 Who is your English teacher? _____

4 What grade are you in? _____

5 When is your birthday? _____

6 Do you like English?　Why or why not?

_____

Let's Plan and Make a Presentation

Task

Our Favorite Things　Conduct a survey and present the results.
テーマを１つ選びアンケート調査をし、その結果を発表しましょう。

Our survey is on favorite fruits / favorite sports / favorite animals.

☐ fruits　　☐ sports　　☐ animals

Our favorite fruits　(What fruit do you like?)

The top three are _____, _____ and _____.

Our favorite sports　(What sport do you like?)

The top three are _____, _____ and _____.

Our favorite animals　(What animal do you like?)

The top three are _____, _____ and _____.

Let's Listen

p.24 の絵を見ながら答えましょう。

Ann	Eve	JJ	Yumi	Nelson	Daisuke	Lisa	Mark	Min	Ema
( )	( )	( )	( )	( )	( )	( )	( )	( )	( )

Animal Talk

32

How do you like my **new** hairstyle?

新しい髪形どう？

It's **cool**!
かっこいい！

It's **nice**!
いいね！

It's **great**!
最高！

It's... **strange**...
ちょっと…ヘン…

まず、使ってみよう！

Let's get started using "Is it big?"

I have a pet.　A big black duck!

It's big. 　It's black.

I like my pet.　A big black duck.

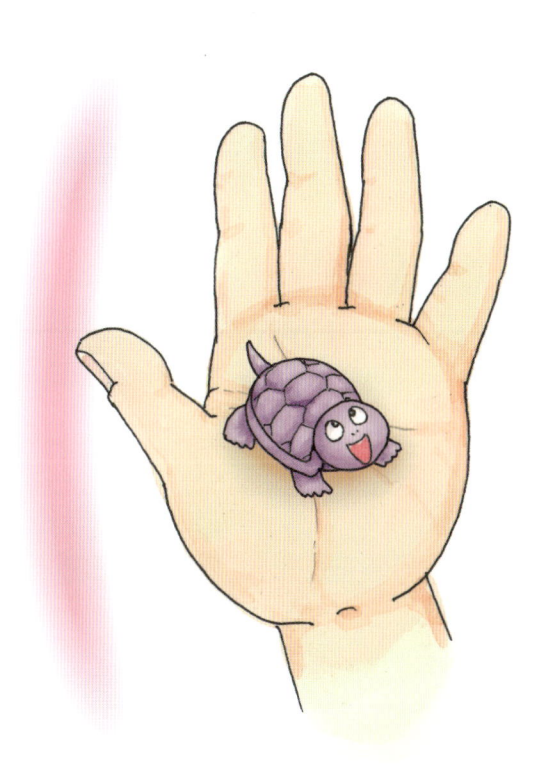

I have a pet.　A little purple turtle.

It's little. 　It's purple.

I like my pet.　A little purple turtle.

■ 人や物の形状、色、状態、数などを言う時は、その言葉のすぐ前に言います。

ただ犬といわれてもねェ。
どんな犬なの？

1	どんなものか（形状、色）	**a big black dog**	（黒くて大きな犬）
2	どんな状態か	**an old dog**	（年老いた犬）
3	数や量を説明	**three dogs**	（3匹の犬）
4	どれか	**that dog**	（あの犬）

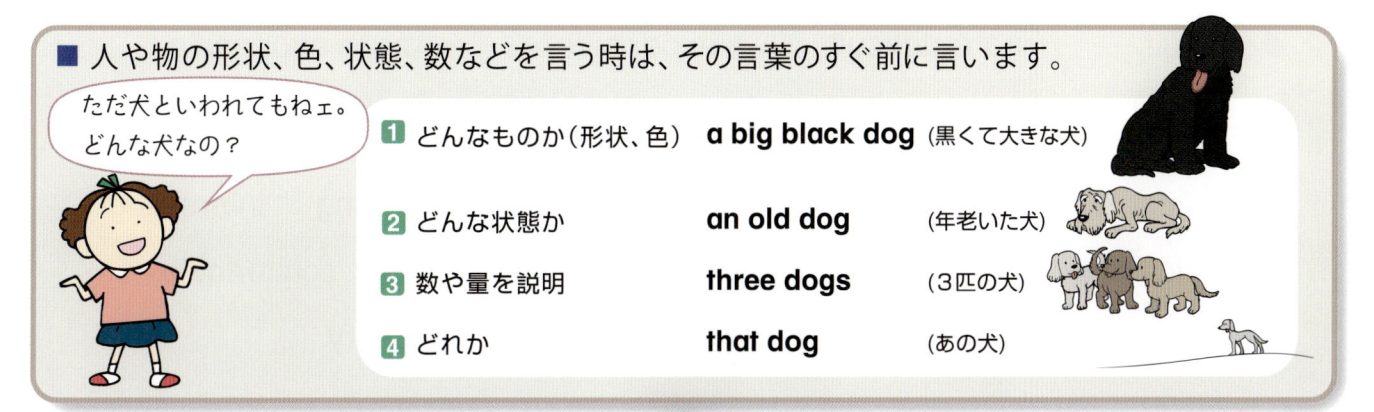

1 形状、色、性質・状態、数などを表す言葉を練習しましょう。

big	small	long	short	round	tiny	large	huge /	blue	brown /
good	bad	young	old	strong	weak	clean	dirty	shiny
hungry	thirsty	healthy	sweet	difficult	easy	correct	wrong	free
happy	sad	angry	funny	tired	busy	noisy	sleepy	sick
brave	gentle	kind	lovely	smart	strict	polite	shy	wise /

one two three some any many / first second third / this that these those

2 1つだけでなく、たくさん続けて言うこともできます。

「いくつか」が1番!　「どんなものか」が2番!　その次は「色」!

数　　どんな　　色

three　　　**beautiful** **big**　　　**yellow**　　　**flowers**

3 説明する言葉が文の最後にくることもあります。

I have a **black** duck.　My duck is **black**.

This is an **expensive** bag.　This bag is **expensive**.

4 「とても〜」と言う時は **very** を付けます。

a bat　　　　a scary bat　　　　a **very** scary bat

5 びっくりした時は **How** を先に言います。「**物や人**」におどろく時は **What** を先に言います。

● beautiful　　　　——→　　**How** beautiful!

● a beautiful flower　——→　**What** a beautiful flower!

One more chant!

35

What a pretty, what a pretty, what a pretty girl I am!
What a rude, what a rude, what a rude boy you are!

What a big dog!

6 「もっと〜だ」と言う時は言葉の後ろに **er** を付けます。言葉は変化せず、**more** を先に言うこともあります。

● young ——→ young**er**　● heavy ——→ heav**ier**　● red ——→ red**der**

● difficult ——→ **more** difficult　● expensive ——→ **more** expensive

7 「**どんな**」ものかを表す言葉として、次の言葉も覚えておきましょう。

famous	strange	quiet	excellent	different	exciting	interesting
boring	important	favorite	wonderful	powerful	useful	comfortable
convenient	dangerous	delicious	friendly	necessary

Complete the sentences.

1 I have a _____ friend. **2** My teacher is _____.

3 _____ is kind. **4** _____ is important.

5 _____ is useful. **6** _____ is interesting.

7 _____ is convenient. **8** _____ is difficult.

9 _____ is strong, but _____ is stronger.

10 _____ is small, but _____ is smaller.

Let's Plan and Make a Presentation

Task

My Opinions Choose 3 items from below. Write four words to describe them.
下の英語の中から3つを選び、その物について思い浮かぶ言葉（1語ずつ）を４つ書きましょう。

● _____ : _____ , _____ ,

_____ ,

● _____ : _____ , _____ ,

_____ ,

● _____ : _____ , _____ ,

_____ ,

school   flowers   clouds   teachers   steak   elephants   the sky

Let's discuss!

Compare and discuss the words you chose with your classmates. 思い浮かんだ言葉の違いを話し合いましょう。

Let's Listen

p.28の1~14の絵を見ながら答えましょう。

1 _____ **2** _____ **3** _____ **4** _____

Animal Talk

36

Mom, **can** you reach?
お母さん、とどく？
I **can't**. ぼくダメそう。

Almost.
もう少し…

まず、使ってみよう！
Let's get started using "Can you …?"

All for one, one for all! What can we do?

JJ
I can cook meals.
I can't take care of the elderly.
I can't clean up the rubble.
I can carry heavy things.
I can't do sign language.

Ann
I can cook meals.
I can't take care of the elderly.
I can clean up the rubble.
I can carry heavy things.
I can do sign language.

Daisuke
I can't cook meals.
I can take care of the elderly.
I can clean up the rubble.
I can't carry heavy things.
I can't do sign language.

Lisa
I can't cook meals.
I can take care of the elderly.
I can't clean up the rubble.
I can carry heavy things.
I can do sign language.

Eve
I can't cook meals.
I can take care of the elderly.
I can clean up the rubble.
I can't carry heavy things.
I can do sign language.

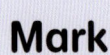

Mark
I can't cook meals.
I can take care of the elderly.
I can't clean up the rubble.
I can carry heavy things.
I can't do sign language.

Mr. Takahashi
I can cook meals.
I can't take care of the elderly.
I can clean up the rubble.
I can carry heavy things.
I can't do sign language.

Ms. Kobayashi
I can cook meals.
I can take care of the elderly.
I can clean up the rubble.
I can carry heavy things.
I can do sign language.

Min
I can cook meals.
I can't take care of the elderly.
I can't clean up the rubble.
I can't carry heavy things.
I can do sign language.

Nelson
I can cook meals.
I can take care of the elderly.
I can clean up the rubble.
I can't carry heavy things.
I can do sign language.

37→38

I can't do it.

Yes, you can.

I can't do it.

Yes, you can.

Try it, try it, you can do it.

I made it, I made it, I made it. All right!

You made it, you made it, you made it. All right!

■ 「〜ができます」と言う時は
can を使います。

ちょっと入れて！

「できる」と言いたい時は、
ぼくが先〜！

え?!

1 「〜ができる」を表す **can** は動作を表す言葉のすぐ前に言います。

| I **can** whistle. | My father **can** whistle. |

canはだれのことにも使えるんだ。

2 「〜ができない」と言う時は **can** の後に **not** を付けます。

| I **cannot** whistle. | My father **cannot** whistle. |

できない

できる

can not = cannot = can't

3 「〜はできますか？」と質問する時は、**Can** で始めます。

| **Can** you whistle? | ● Yes, I **can**. |
| | ● No, I **can't**. |

One more chant!

 39

Can you swim? Can you swim? Yes, I can. Yes, I can.
Can you ski? Can you ski? No, I can't. No, I can't.

4 「何ができますか？」と質問する時は **What**、「だれができますか？」と質問する時は **Who** で始めます。

| **What** can you do? | ● I can **ride a unicycle**. |
| **Who** can answer the question? | ● **I** can. |

5 **can** を使って「〜してもよい」を表すこともあります。**may** も「〜してよい」という意味で使えます。

| **Can I** come in? |
| **Can I** have two hamburgers, please? |

| **May I** sit here? | ● Yes, you **may**. |
| | ● No, you **may not**. |

May I come in?
入ってもよいですか？

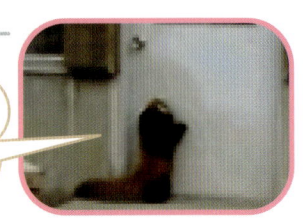

● **can't be** で「〜のはずがない」という意味になるよ！

Wow! It can't be true!
うっそ〜！

6 **can** の過去形 **could** を使って「〜していただけますか？」とていねいに頼む表現を覚えましょう。

| **Could you** tell me your email address? | Emailアドレスを教えていただけますか？ |
| **Could you** do me a favor? | お願いがあるのですが。 |

● **I wish I could...** で今はできないけれど「〜できたらいいな」という意味になるんだって！

I wish I could fly.
飛べたらな〜

■ Write each sentence. If they are not true for you, rewrite them using "not".

1 I can use an abacus.

2 I can play the recorder.

3 I can wink with both eyes.

4 I can moonwalk.

5 I can read music.

6 I can count from one to three in more than three languages.

Let's Plan and Make a Presentation

Task

Our Robot Let's make a robot that can make elderly people happy. What can it do?
お年寄りに喜ばれる便利なロボットを作りましょう。

My Idea My robot can _____.

Group Summary

This is our robot.

It can _____.

It can _____.

Draw a robot.

It can _____.

Let's Listen

p.32 の絵（一番下の4人は除く）を見ながら答えましょう。

Eve	JJ	Ann	Daisuke	Lisa	Mark
( )	( )	( )	( )	( )	( )

Animal Talk

40

You **are** wearing nice pants!

ステキなパンツはいてるね！

No. **I'm** not wearing pants. The stripes are natural.

ううん、パンツじゃないよ。
これ、天然もの。

まず、使ってみよう！

Let's get started using "I am …ing."

I am dancing. You are dancing.

He is dancing. She is dancing.

They are dancing.

We are dancing on the earth.

Look! It is dancing, too!

eating   walking   reading

■「今〜しています」と言う時は、Be ファミリー（**am, is, are**）＋動作を表す言葉＋**ing** で表します。

私たちも
大切なんだからね！

am is are ＋ walk ing

ing がくっつくと、
「〜している」という意味です。

1 今していること を Be ファミリー **(am, is, are)** + **…ing** を付けて練習しましょう。

 **One more chant!**

43

Read! I'm reading. Write! I'm writing. Study! I'm studying.
Sit! I'm sitting. Listen! I'm listening to you!

ing を書く時は、つづり方に注意が必要な言葉もあります。

I am **eating**.	I am **washing**.	I am **crying**.	I am **thinking**.
I am **dancing**.	I am **driving**.	I am **smiling**.	I am **coming**.
I am **running**.	I am **hopping**.	I am **swimming**.	I am **chatting**.

はやく〜！

待って〜！

ぼくを忘れないで〜！

2 「〜していますか？」と質問する時と、「〜(今)していません」の言い方を練習しましょう。

Are you **sleeping?**

No, I am **not**. I am **not** sleeping.
I am **studying**.

Are you kidding?
うっそ〜！

3 「何をしていますか？」と質問する時は **What** で始めます。その他、次の表現を練習しましょう。

What are you doing?	I am studying English.
Where are you going?	I am going to school.
Who is playing the piano?	My mother is.

4 もともと行為が続いている状態を表す言葉は、**ing** を付ける必要はありません。

I **like** music.	I **live** in Hokkaido.	I **want** a dog.
I **know** Mr. Miller.	I **love** my pet.	I **have** a sister.

● **have** のいろいろ

私は状態を表す**have**だから**ing**は付けないの。

● I **have** a sister.　（いる）
● I **have** a book.　（持っている）
● I **have** a dog.　（飼っている）

私たちは動作を表すから Be ファミリーと一緒になって「〜している」という意味になりまーす。

● I **am having** lunch now.
● We **are having** a good time.

5 近い未来をBeファミリー＋**…ing**で表す時もあります。

I **am leaving** for Hawaii tomorrow.
I **am taking** a test tomorrow.
When **is** your mother **coming**?

● 次の表現も覚えておくと便利です。

● I'm coming.
● I'm starving.
● The phone is ringing.

■ Write each sentence. If they are not true for you, rewrite them using "not".

1 I am studying English now.

2 It is raining now.

3 My teacher is wearing contact lenses now.

4 I am writing now.

5 I am enjoying my school life.

6 I live in Kyushu.

7 I know my teacher's birthday.

Let's Plan and Make a Presentation

Task

The Best Excuses Your mother asks you to help her, but you think you are busy! What are you doing?
お母さんが手伝ってくれるように頼んでいます。手伝わなくても許されそうな言い訳は？

Mother: Will you come and help me right now?

Ex. Sorry, I can't because I am ___talking on the phone___ now.

My Idea Sorry, I can't because I am _____ now.

Group Summary

❶ Sorry, I can't because I am _____ now.

❷ Sorry, I can't because I am _____ now.

❸ Sorry, I can't because I am _____ now.

 **Let's Listen**

p.36の絵を見ながら答えましょう。

■1 _____ ■2 _____ ■3 _____ ■4 _____

Animal Talk
44

Does this dog eat cats?
この犬… ネコ食べたりする？

I hope it doesn't.
それはない… と思うけど。

Relax.
I'm not hungry now.
大丈夫。今おなかすいてないし。

まず、使ってみよう！
Let's get started using "Lisa's house has…"

1 （　　　　　　）

2 （　　　　　　）

3 （　　　　　　）

4 （　　　　　　）

5 （　　　　　　）

6 （　　　　　　）

7 （　　　　　　）

8 （　　　　　　）

45→46

Do you like me?   No, we don't.

Yes, you do.   No, we don't.

Yes, you do.   No, we don't.

Yes, you do.   All right, we like you.

Does he like me?   No, he doesn't.

Yes, he does.   No, he doesn't.

Yes, he does.   No, he doesn't.

Yes, he does.   All right, he likes you.

Does she like me?   No, she doesn't.

Yes, she does.   No, she doesn't.

Yes, she does.   No, she doesn't.

Yes, she does.   All right, she likes you.

■ 話す人、聞く人以外のこと（単数）を話題にする時、英語では動作を表す言葉が変化します。

1 I, You, We, They の時は **have** だけど、He, She, It の時は **has** に変身します。

話す人が1番目の人、話し相手（聞く人）が2番目の人、話題になる人や物は3番目なので、「3人称」と言います。

 話す人 I have

 聞く人 You have

 話題になる人, 物
男ならば **He**
女ならば **She** } **has**
物ならば **It**

話す人が2人以上ならば
We have

聞く人が2人以上ならば
You have

話題になる人が2人以上ならば
They have

 **One more chant!**
47

You have a tail. He has a tail. She has a tail. It has a tail.
They all have one, but I don't.

2 He, She, It の時の形を音に注意して練習しましょう。言葉のつづり方にも気を付けましょう。

run → run**s**	come → come**s**	read → read**s**
walk → walk**s**	help → help**s**	speak → speak**s**
want → want**s**	write → write**s**	eat → eat**s**
use → use**s**	lose → lose**s**	choose → choose**s**
study → stud**ies**	fly → fl**ies**	cry → cr**ies**
wash → wash**es**	teach → teach**es**	go → go**es**
＊have → ha**s**	do → do**es**	say → say**s**

3 質問する時、「～しない」と言う時
He, She, It の時は **do** の代わりに **does** を使います。

 ぼくがお手伝いします。
sは追い出しますのでご安心を！ does

He **lives** in Tokyo.

Does he **live**~~s~~ in Tokyo?　Sはいりません！

● Yes, he **does**.
● No, he **doesn't**.
does not = doesn't

He **doesn't live**~~s~~ in Tokyo.
Sは必要ありません。

4 what, where, when, how, why, who を使って、話題になっている人のことを質問する時

何を？	トムはほしいの？	**What** does Tom want?
どこに？	トムは住んでいるの？	**Where** does Tom live?
いつ？	トムは帰ってくるの？	**When** does Tom come home?
どうやって？	トムは帰ってくるの？	**How** does Tom come home?
なぜ？	トムはそれがほしいの？	**Why** does Tom want that?

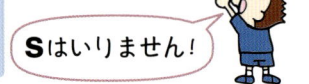 Who
Who の時はだれ（主語）がわからないので、後は質問文の形になりません。

| だれが？ | ピアノを弾くの？ | **Who** plays the piano?　My father **does**. |
| | | I **do**. |

1 Write each sentence. If they are not true for you, rewrite them using "not".

1 Santa Claus comes to my house.

2 My mother drives a car.

3 February has twenty-nine days this year.

4 The moon is full this week.

2 Answer the questions.

Ex. Does your father smoke?   No, he doesn't. He doesn't smoke.   Yes, he does. He smokes.

1 Does your school have a swimming pool?

2 When does the school year start in Japan?

Let's Plan and Make a Presentation

Famous People   Choose a currently famous person, and describe his/her job and life.
今活躍している有名な人を１人選び、その人のことを紹介しましょう。

Task

What's his/her name? _____.

He/ She is a _____.
(occupation)

He/ She _____.

He/ She _____.

He/ She _____.

I like him / her because _____

_____.

Let's Listen

p.40 の絵を見ながら答えましょう。

1 _____   **2** _____   **3** _____   **4** _____

Animal Talk

48

Woohoo! ヤッホー!
There is a squirrel
on a dog!

犬の上にリスがいまーす!

You're annoying. ウザイんだけど…

Don't hang around. まとわりつかないで。

Get off! 降りてよ!

まず、使ってみよう!

Let's get started using "There is ... There are ..."

Where's my pencil? Where's my pencil? On？ In？ Under？

On the desk? In the desk? Under the desk? Where? ××××

Is it blue? Is it green? Is it red or black?

Where's my pencil? Where's my pencil? On? In? Under?

■ 場所をはっきり言いたい時は、上、下など場所を表す言葉を先に言います。

desk のところにあったよ。

ただ、机のところと言われてもね。
「机の上なの？」「下なの？」
「そばなの？」「中なの？」

Desk?　**On** the desk?

Under the desk?

By the desk?

In the desk?

1 いろいろな「**場所**」を表す言葉を練習しましょう。

on the bench   **in** the lake   **under** the bench   **over** the mountain
between the trees   **by** the lake   **in front of** the cottage   **behind** the tree

2 「**時・期間・手段・方向**」などを表す言葉を練習しましょう。

at three o'clock   **at** night   **around** three o'clock   **in** the morning   **on** Sunday   **on** July 20th
in April   **in** 2020 /   **for** six hours   **before** ten   **after** ten   **between** eight and ten
until 10:30   **by** 10:30 /   **by** bike   **in** English /   **to** the park   **for** Tokyo /   **with** my friends

I get up **around** six o'clock **in** the morning.
I go to school **by** bus **with** my sister.
The bus is bound **for** Shinjuku. I get off the bus **at** Midorigaoka.
My school is **in front of** City Hall.
At night, I keep a diary **in** English.
I usually take a bath **between** eight and nine.
I watch the news on TV **until** 9:30 pm.
I go to bed **by** ten o'clock. I usually sleep **for** eight hours.

3 「〜があります」「〜がいます」と言いたい時は **There is/ There are** で始めます。

There is a big park in my town.

質問する時は
Is there a big park in your town?

答え方は
Yes, there **is**.   No, there **isn't**.

There are twenty-four hour**s** in a day.

質問する時は
Are there twenty-four hour**s** in a day?

答え方は
Yes, there **are**.   No, there **aren't**.

「〜があります」「〜がいます」と言う時は、ぼくが案内します。ついてきてくださ〜い。

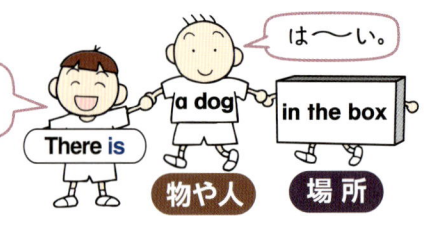
は〜い。
There is / a dog / in the box
物や人　場所

There is a dog in the bag.

One more chant!
51
There is a cow between the trees. There is a fox under the tree.
There is a monkey in the tree. There is a pig by the tree.
There are birds over the tree. There are ducks in front of the tree.

■ Write your own answers.

1 What time do you get up in the morning?

_____

2 How do you come to school?

_____

3 Do you come to school with your friends?

_____

4 Do you do your homework before or after supper?

_____

5 How many hours do you usually sleep in a day?

_____

6 How many students are there in your class?

_____

Let's Plan and Make a Presentation

Task

My Routine and Future Plans Write about your daily routine and your plans for the future.
あなたが日常にしていることと、未来への決意を書きましょう。

My Routine

● I _____ **in** the morning.

● I _____ **by** five o'clock in the evening.

● I _____ **after** dinner.

● I _____ **around** nine o'clock.

● I _____ **on** Sunday morning.

My Plan

● I will _____ **in** a year.

● I will _____ **by** the year 2040.

Let's Listen

p.44 の 1~6 の絵を見ながら答えましょう。

■1 ⬭ ■2 ⬭ ■3 ⬭ ■4 ⬭

Animal Talk

🔵52

Please walk **slowly**, Mom.
お母さん、ゆっくり歩いてね。

Hold on **tight**, baby.
ぼうや、しっかり私につかまるのよ。

まず、使ってみよう!
Let's get started using "early, easily, loudly"

1 Find　　someone　who　　gets up early.

gets up early.

2 Find　　someone　who　　gets tired easily.

gets tired easily.

3 Find　　someone　who　　can whistle loudly.

can whistle loudly.

4 Find　　someone　who　　likes spicy food very much.

likes spicy food very much.

5 Find　　someone　who　　rides a bicycle every day.

rides a bicycle every day.

6 Find　　someone　who　　always stays up late.

always stays up late.

7 Find　　someone　who　　sees his/her grandparents regularly.

sees his/her grandparents regularly.

Happily happily happily.   Sing happily please.

Loudly loudly loudly.   Sing loudly please.

Gently gently gently.   Sing gently please.

Clearly clearly clearly.   Sing clearly please.

Slowly slowly slowly.   Sing slowly please.

Softly softly softly.   Sing softly please.

■ 動作の様子を表す言葉(どのように?)は、ふつう動作のすぐ後ろに付けます。

run fast

run slowly

run

1 「**動作をくわしく言う**」言葉を覚えましょう。

well	You speak English **well**.
slowly	My grandmother walks **slowly**.
hard	My brother studies **hard**.
carefully	Open the box **carefully**.
early	I get up **early** in the morning.
late	Don't stay up **late**.
happily	Smile **happily**.
fast	He can run **fast**.

2 「**いつ**」「**どこで**」「**どのくらい**」（時、場所、程度）を表す言葉

● 「**時**」

See you **soon**.

Do it **now**.

I met the man two days **ago**.

My father came home at **eight o'clock** **last night**.

小さい単位が先にくるよ！

● 「**場所**」

I want to go **abroad**.

I'm **here**. He's **there**.

Go **upstairs**.

I will be **home** by five.

● 「**程度**」

He can run **very** fast.

I like English **very much**.

That castle is **very** old.

その他、決まった言い方があるので丸ごと覚えましょう。

I am from Japan. Me, **too**. 　私もです。

I don't like fish. I don't **either**. 　私も（好きではない）です。

I love pop music. **So** do I. 　私も（好き）です。

I guess **so**. I hope **so**. 　そう思います。そう願っています。

3 「**どのくらいの割合で**」（頻度）を表す言葉

● 頻度を表す言葉は、**Be** ファミリー（**am, is, are**）の後ろ、動作を表す言葉の前に言います。

You are **always** kind.　　I **always** help my mother.

never			sometimes	often	usually	always
0%			50%	60%	80%	100%

One more chant!

55

You stay up late. You always stay up late. You stay up late. You always stay up late. You are mad. You are always mad. You are mad. You are always mad at me!

4 「**〜すぎる**」と言う時は **too** を使います。

● young → too young　　● big → too big　　● expensive → too expensive

● fast → too fast　　● slowly → too slowly　　● loudly → too loudly

5 「**もっと〜**」と言う時は **er** または **more** を付けます。

Study **hard**.　　⟹　　Study **harder**.

Listen **carefully**.　　⟹　　Listen **more** **carefully**.

■ Complete the sentences using the words below.

1 I usually eat _____.   **2** I usually speak _____.

3 I always write _____.   **4** My teacher speaks _____.

5 My mother sometimes gets up _____.

6 Pandas run very _____.

| fast   slowly   late   early   quietly   loudly   gently   clearly   poorly   neatly |

7 I _____ study before dinner.   **8** I _____ clean my room.

9 I _____ cook for my family.   **10** I _____ stay up late.

| never   sometimes   often   usually   always |

Let's Plan and Make a Presentation

Task

We are proud of you!   Who runs fast? Who sings well? Who do you think?

クラスのいろいろな一番を探してみましょう。グループで話し合って上位3人を発表しましょう。

My Idea

● _____ runs fast. _____ sings well.

● _____ is always kind to everyone. _____ is always happy.

Group Summary

● _____ , _____ and _____ run fast.

● _____ , _____ and _____ sing well.

● _____ , _____ and _____ are always kind to everyone.

● _____ , _____ and _____ are always happy.

Let's Listen

1	**2**	**3**	**4**
a. Yumi	**a.** Eve	**a.** Ann	**a.** running
b. Ann	**b.** JJ	**b.** Ema	**b.** walking fast
c. Daisuke	**c.** Nelson	**c.** JJ	**c.** walking slowly

Animal Talk

56

You **will be** late.
Go, go!

遅れちゃうよー。行け行け〜！

Okay...
I **will** do my best.

うん。がんばるよ…

まず、使ってみよう！

Let's get started using "What will ... do?"

What will you do in order to be a good speaker of English?

JJ	
Ann	
Daisuke	
Lisa	
Nelson	
Eve	

Let's Chant!

57→58

It's a sunny day today. What will you do?

I will go swimming.

And I will eat lunch on the beach.

It's a rainy day today. What will you do?

I will stay home.

And I will read a book on the bed.

It's a snowy day today. What will you do?

I will go outside.

And I will take a walk in the park.

■ これから「**すること**」「**起こること**」は **will** を使って言います。

ちょっと入れて！

「これから」のことを言いたい時は、ぼくがいる〜！

え?!

I will study

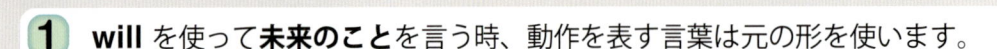

1 **will** を使って**未来のこと**を言う時、動作を表す言葉は元の形を使います。

未来のぼくが来たからには
ちゃんと元の形に戻してね。

es を取って
元の go に戻ったよ。

Be ファミリーの一員
だからam も is も are も
元の形は be でーす！

え？元の形って何？

He **will go** to the moon.　　He **will be** an astronaut.

2 **will** を付けて練習しましょう。

I **will** study this evening.　　I **will be** late for class.

She **will** catch up.　　You **will be** all right.

It **will** rain tomorrow.　　He **will be** a scientist.

We **will** sing a song.　　We **will be** thirteen years old next year.

I will = I'll　　You will = You'll

One more chant!

59

I'll get it. I'll do it. I'll go first. I'll be home soon and I'll call you back.

3 **質問する** 時と「**〜ではないでしょう**」と言う時

will not = won't

ぼくたちが一緒に
なった時は読み方
に注意。

Will it rain tomorrow?

Yes, it **will**.　　No, it **won't** (**will not**).

It **won't** (**will not**) rain tomorrow.　It **will** be fine.

4 **be (am, is, are) going to** もこれからのことを表します。

I **am going to** study this evening.

ぼくたちも一緒になってこれからのことを表すんだよ。

One more chant!

60

What are you going to do?　read

What are you going to do today?　buy

What are you going to do?　have

5 **will** は「これからのこと」を言う時だけでなく、「お願いする時」にも使います。

人にお願いしたり、誘ったりする時もぼくがいるのさ。

Will you help me?　　No problem.

Will you come with me?　　Sure.

Write each sentence. If they are not true for you, rewrite them using "not".

1 It will rain tomorrow.

2 I will take a bath tonight.

3 I will be home by five.

4 I will do my homework before supper.

5 There will be an interesting program on TV tonight.

6 My family will go out for dinner this weekend.

Let's Plan and Make a Presentation

Task

In Twenty Years Imagine what your life and society will be like in 20 years.
20年後の自分と社会を想像して発表しましょう。

In twenty years, I will be _____ years old.

☐ I will be married.   ☐ I will have children.   ☐ I will be rich.
☐ I will live in a foreign country.   ☐ I will still live in the same city.

I will _____.

☐ People will find aliens on another planet.
☐ There will be no wars.
☐ There will be a shuttle flight between the earth and the moon.
☐ There will be flying bicycles.

There will be _____.

Let's Listen

1	**2**	**3**	**4**
a. nothing	a. park	a. Sky Tree	a. scientist
b. library	b. sunny	b. aquarium	b. doctor
c. Jenny	c. rainy	c. aunt	c. teacher

61

Mirror, mirror,
かがみよ、かがみ。

who is **the most beautiful** lady in the world?
世界で一番美しい女性はだれだ。

Queen, you are **beautiful**.
女王様あなたは美しいです。

But Snow White is **more beautiful** than you.
でも白雪姫はもっと美しい。

まず、使ってみよう!

Let's get started using "Are you taller than … ?"

Daisuke   Jason   JJ

Lisa   Ann   Eve

62➔63

This one is big, bigger than the other one.

This one is cheap, cheaper than the other one.

This one is nice, nicer than the other one.

Big, bigger

cheap, cheaper

nice, nicer

I'll take the better one.

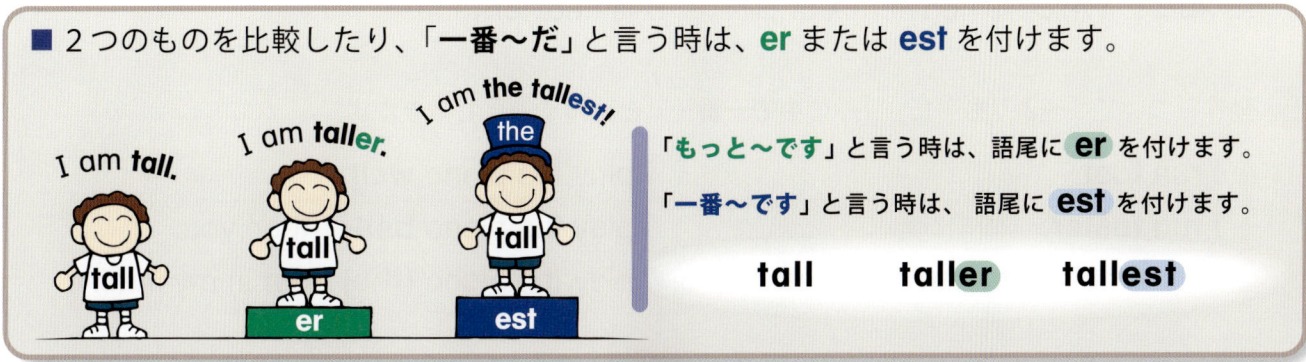

■ 2つのものを比較したり、「一番〜だ」と言う時は、er または est を付けます。

I am tall.

I am taller.

I am the tallest!

「もっと〜です」と言う時は、語尾に er を付けます。

「一番〜です」と言う時は、語尾に est を付けます。

tall　　taller　　tallest

1 「より…だ」「〜の中で一番…」の言い方を練習しましょう。

● **er** **est** が付くグループ

old → older → the oldest	easy → easier → the easiest
big → bigger → the biggest	large → larger → the largest
happy → happier → the happiest	pretty → prettier → the prettiest

● 全く変身グループ

| good → better → the best | bad → worse → the worst |

● **more** **most** が付くグループ

| interesting → **more** interesting → the **most** interesting |
| difficult → **more** difficult → the **most** difficult |
| famous → **more** famous → the **most** famous |
| popular → **more** popular → the **most** popular |

一番の時、**the** を忘れないで〜。

est

🎵 **One more chant!**

64

I am happy. I am happier. I am the happiest.
I am pretty. I am prettier. I am the prettiest.

2 「〜よりも…だ」と言う時は **er** の後に **than 〜** を続けて言います。

| I am strong. ➡ | I am strong**er than you**. |
| I am tall. ➡ | I am tall**er than my brother**. |

3 「〜の中で一番」と言う時、(人)数の中では **of**、グループ(容器)の中で一番の時は **in** を使います。

I am **the** tall**est of** the three.
I am **the** tall**est in** my class.

I am **the** young**est of** the three.
I am **the** young**est in** my family.
My house is **the** strong**est of** the three.

4 「**A**と**B**のどちらが、より〜ですか」と質問したい時は **A or B** を使います。

人の場合： Who is taller, A **or** B?　　A is taller than B.

物の場合： Which is heavier, A **or** B?　　B is heavier than A.

5 動作について「〜よりも…だ」「〜の中で一番…」と比べることもできます。

I run **fast**.	I play the piano **well**.
I run **faster**.	I play the piano **better** than you.
I run **(the) fastest** in my class.	I play the piano **(the) best** in my family.

Let's Write

▪ Complete the sentences.

1 The moon is ＿＿＿＿＿＿＿＿＿＿＿ than the earth. (smaller or bigger)

2 One inch is ＿＿＿＿＿＿＿＿＿＿＿ than one centimeter. (longer or shorter)

3 I am ＿＿＿＿＿＿＿＿＿＿＿ than my mother. (taller or shorter)

4 Cheetahs run ＿＿＿＿＿＿＿＿＿＿＿ than the Shinkansen. (faster or slower)

5 I like ＿＿＿＿＿＿＿＿＿ better than ＿＿＿＿＿＿＿＿＿.

6 The best athlete in my class is ＿＿＿＿＿＿＿＿＿.

7 ＿＿＿＿＿＿＿＿＿ is the most difficult subject for me.

Let's Plan and Make a Presentation

Animals in the World   What animals are the cutest? The scariest? Present your opinion.
あなたにとって一番かわいい動物は？一番怖い動物は？動物についてスピーチしましょう。

Among all the animals in the world,

I think ＿＿＿＿＿＿＿＿＿＿＿ are the cutest.

＿＿＿＿＿＿＿＿＿＿＿ are the scariest.

＿＿＿＿＿＿＿＿＿＿＿ are the strongest.

＿＿＿＿＿＿＿＿＿＿＿ are the funniest.

＿＿＿＿＿＿＿＿＿＿＿ are the most beautiful.

In Japan, ＿＿＿＿＿＿＿＿＿ are the most popular animals.

))) Let's Listen

p.56の絵を見ながら答えましょう。

Daisuke ( )   Jason ( )   JJ ( )   Lisa ( )   Ann ( )   Eve ( )

Animal Talk

65

What happened?

いったいどうしたの？

I was just going down the slide.

ただ、滑り台をすべっていただけなのに。

まず、使ってみよう！

Let's get started using "What was ... doing?"

	JJ	Eve
8 o'clock in the morning		
10 : 30 in the morning		
12 : 30 in the afternoon		
3 o'clock in the afternoon		
7 o'clock in the evening		
10 o'clock at night		

Let's Chant !

Busy, busy, busy.

We were busy all day long.

Mom was cooking all day long.

Dad was shopping all day long.

I was washing all day long.

Jason was cleaning all day long.

Mary was crying all day long.

Zippy was running all day long.

Busy, busy, busy.

We were busy all day long.

■ 過去の状態を言う時は **Be** ファミリー（**am, is, are**）の **was, were** を使います。

I, he, she, it の時は **was**、
you（あなた / あなたたち）**, we, they** の時は **were** を
使います。

え、ぼくたちも Be ファミリーだったの？

was   were

1 過去の状態を「現在」「未来」の状態と共に、時の流れの順に練習しましょう。

 過去のことは、われわれ2人にお任せください。  現在のことは、私たち3人がおせわします。  未来のことは、ぼく1人でがんばります！！

I **was** tired yesterday.

I **am** sleepy now.

I **will be** fine tomorrow.

It **was** rainy yesterday.

It **is** cloudy today.

It **will be** sunny tomorrow.

 **One more chant!**

68

It was rainy. It is cloudy.   It will be sunny soon. (×2)

2 過去の状態を「〜だった？」と質問する時、「〜ではなかった」と言う時

You **were** busy.

Were you busy?

Yes, I **was**.   No, I **wasn't**.

I **was not** busy at that time.

You **were not** busy.

He **was not** busy.

were not = weren't
was not = wasn't

（at that time ＝その当時）

3 「〜していました」と言う時は、**was, were** ＋動作を表す言葉＋**ing** で言います。

I **was** watch**ing** TV.

He **was** read**ing** the newspaper.

My father **was** sleep**ing** on the sofa.

My mother and I **were** cook**ing** in the kitchen.

4 過去にしていたことを「〜してた？」と質問する時、「〜していなかった」と言う時

You **were** watch**ing** TV.

Were you watch**ing** TV?

Yes, I **was**. No, I **wasn't**.

I **was not** watch**ing** TV at that time.

You **were not** watch**ing** TV.

He **was not** watch**ing** TV.

5 **What, Where, When, Who, Why** を使って**過去の状態、過去にしていたこと**を質問しましょう。

Where **were** you yesterday?

When **was** your English exam?

Who **was** absent last week?

Why **were** you late?

What **were** you do**ing** yesterday?

Who **was** sing**ing**?

Why **was** she cry**ing**?

Where **was** he go**ing**?

Write each sentence. If they are not true for you, rewrite them using "not".

1 It was fine yesterday.

2 My teacher was absent from school yesterday.

3 The last English test was easy.

4 I was sick in bed last week.

5 I was studying at nine o'clock last night.

6 Today's breakfast was delicious.

7 I was sleeping at ten o'clock last night.

Let's Plan and Make a Presentation

Task

Past, Present and Future Write what you did in the past, are doing now, and will do in the future.
昨夜、今、明日の朝の時間の流れの中であなたの行動を書いてみましょう。

Where were you at eight o'clock last night? _____

What were you doing at that time? _____

Where are you now? _____

What are you doing now? _____

Where will you be at ten o'clock tomorrow morning?

_____

What will you be doing then?

_____

Let's Listen

1
a. studying math
b. taking a test
c. watching TV

2
a. talking on the phone
b. washing his dad's car
c. playing with his friends

3
a. watching TV
b. taking a shower
c. an earthquake

4
a. playing in the tent
b. swimming in the lake
c. fishing in the lake

Animal Talk

69

Did you eat my nuts?

ぼくの木の実食べた？

No, I didn't. No way!

食べてなんかいないよ。

Burp! Excuse me!

げっぷ 失礼！

まず、使ってみよう！

Let's get started using "Did you ...?"

1 last night

2 the day before yesterday

3 three days ago

4 four days ago

5 five days ago

6 last Friday

7 yesterday afternoon

8 last Sunday

70→71

Did you make your bed?

Yes, I did. Yes, I did.
I made my bed. Look!

Did you eat your lunch?

Yes, I did. Yes, I did.
I ate my lunch. Look!

Did you clean your room?

Yes, I did. Yes, I did.
I cleaned my room. Look!

Did you take a bath?

Yes, I did. Yes, I did.
I took a bath. Look!

■ 過去のことを言う時、動作を表す言葉は変化します。
　後ろに **ed** が付く時と、全く変身する時があります。

ぼくは **ed** が付くんだよ。　　　へー、私は **d** が付くだけ。　　　ぼくは **went** になるんだ！　　　私は **saw** になるんだもん！

answer ed　　　love d　　　go　　　see
アンサーくん　　　ラブちゃん　　　ごうくん　　　しーちゃん

1 **過去のこと**を言う時、動作を表す言葉は変化します。

play	play**ed**	open	open**ed**	clean	clean**ed**
live	live**d**	love	love**d**	smile	smile**d**
study	stud**ied**	cry	cr**ied**	try	tr**ied**
walk	walk**ed**	wash	wash**ed**	watch	watch**ed**
want	want**ed**	visit	visit**ed**	start	start**ed**
stop	stop**ped**	drop	drop**ped**	plan	plan**ned**

言葉によって音や書き方が変わるので注意しなくちゃ！

一緒にいようね！

もともと動詞の最後に **e** があるから **d** だけでいいよ。

ぼくの場合は最後の字（**p**）がもう1ついるんだ。

私は **y** が **i** に変身してからです。

ぼくたちは全く変身してしまうのです。

run	**ran**	come	**came**	see	**saw**	go	**went**
do	**did**	eat	**ate**	give	**gave**	take	**took**
speak	**spoke**	write	**wrote**	drink	**drank**	choose	**chose**
have	**had**	meet	**met**	make	**made**	sit	**sat**
find	**found**	tell	**told**	leave	**left**	win	**won**
buy	**bought**	teach	**taught**	catch	**caught**	bring	**brought**
cut	**cut**	put	**put**	set	**set**	read	**read**

みんな、ややこしいのね。私たちは変身しません。

ふふふ

2 動作を表す言葉の過去形はだれのことを言っても同じ形です。

 **One more chant!**

72

過去形もいいところあるじゃない。

Who came here? ×××
I came, you came, he came, she came, it came, they came,
Sam came, too! We all came here! ×××

3 **質問する時**、「〜しなかった」と言う時は **did** を使います。

ひかえおろー！
これが目に入らぬか！
did でござるぞ。
元の形に戻れ‼

He **went** to school yesterday.

Did he **go** to school yesterday?

He **did** not **go** to school yesterday.
(didn't)

did not = didn't

4 過去形を使っていろいろなことを質問してみましょう。

 **One more chant!**

73

Where did you go?	I went to the market.
What did you see?	I saw some fruit.
What did you buy?	I bought an apple.
How much did you pay?	I paid a dollar.
What did you do, then?	I ate the apple.

Remember what you did yesterday, and write each sentence.
If they are not true for you, rewrite them using "not".

1 I got up early in the morning.

2 I left home before seven o'clock in the morning.

3 I went to bed after ten.

4 I read the newspaper.

5 I took a bath.

6 It rained.

Let's Plan and Make a Presentation

Task

Historical Figures   Choose a historical person, and describe what he/she did.
歴史上の人物を１人選び、その人のことを紹介しましょう。

My Idea

Name of the person: _____

What he/she did: _____

Group Summary

We chose _____

Let's Listen

p.64 の絵を見ながら答えましょう。

1 ⬭   **2** ⬭   **3** ⬭   **4** ⬭

Animal Talk

74

> **I want to stand on my head.**
> 逆立ちしたいんだけど。

> **Go ahead and try!**
> やってごらんよ！

> **...Standing on one's head is hard.**
> 逆立ちって難しい…

まず、使ってみよう！

Let's get started using "What ... like doing?"

JJ

I like _____

I want to _____

I'm looking forward to _____

Daisuke

I like _____

I want to _____

I'm looking forward to _____

Ann

I like _____

I want to _____

I'm looking forward to _____

Lisa

I like _____

I want to _____

I'm looking forward to _____

 **Let's Chant!**

I like playing games. 👏👏

I like playing games. 👏👏

We like playing, playing games.

How about playing, playing games?

Let's enjoy playing games.

Playing games is so much fun!

Stop playing the game!

■「〜すること」と言う時は、「動作を表す言葉＋**ing**」または「**to**＋動作を表す言葉」で表します。

一緒になると「歩くこと」になるんだよ。

walk ing

to walk

1 〜ing を動作を表す言葉に付けて練習しましょう。

One more chant!

77

We like walking, walking in the park.
We like camping, camping in the woods.
We like fishing, fishing in the river.

〜することは…	**Using** smartphones is prohibited here.
〜するのをやめなさい	**Stop chatting**!
〜する練習をする	I have to **practice speaking** English every day.
〜するのを楽しむ	I **enjoyed talking** with you.
〜し続ける	Let's **keep walking**.
〜しに行く	I **went shopping**.
〜するのを楽しみにする	I am **looking forward to seeing** you again.
〜するのが得意	I **am good at playing** tennis.
〜するのはいかが?	**How about having** a cup of tea?
〜してくれてありがとう	**Thank you for helping** me.
〜し始める	It **started raining**.

2 動作を表す言葉の前に **to** を付ける言い方を練習しましょう。

One more chant!

78

We want to walk, walk in the park.
We want to camp, camp in the woods.
We want to fish, fish in the river.

〜したい	I **want to** have a break.
〜しようと決める	I **decided to** study hard.
〜したいと思う	I **hope to** see you again.
〜になりたい	I **want to be** a doctor.
…は〜することです	My dream **is to** travel around the world.
〜することは…	**It** is easy/difficult **to** make friends.

3 同じ「〜すること」という意味でも動作を表す言葉によって異なる場合があります。

ぼくは **to** と一緒でないとイヤ！

want to swim

I want **to swim.**

ぼくは **ing** とでないとイヤ！

enjoy swimming

He enjoyed **swimming.**

私はどちらとも仲良しです。

like swimming to swim

I like **swimming.**

I like **to swim.**

■ Write each sentence. If they are not true for you, rewrite them using "not".

1 I like reading mystery books.

2 I enjoy studying English.

3 Studying English is important for our future.

4 I want to be rich.

5 My dream is to live in Hawaii.

6 I want to sit in the first row in the classroom.

Let's Plan and Make a Presentation

Task

My favorite Things to Do   What activities are fun? Write about your ideas.
あなたにとって好きなこと、得意なことは？あなた自身の考えを書きましょう。

I enjoy _____ at school. I enjoy _____ at home.

I am good at _____ .

It is great to _____ .

It is fun to _____ .

My dream is to _____ .

 Let's Listen

1	**2**	**3**	**4**
a. have a cup of tea	a. the pool	a. It's easy.	a. at the front
b. bake cookies	b. the ocean	b. It's fun.	b. can't see the board
c. eat cookies	c. an aquarium	c. It's boring.	c. wearing glasses

Animal Talk

79

I am freezing. ぼく、凍えています。
Please give me **something to wear**.
何か着るものをください。
And **something hot to drink**, too.
それと何か温かい飲み物も。

まず、使ってみよう！
Let's get started using "Is it something to…?"

earrings

map

noodle soup

coffee

hat

curry

cocoa

sneakers

wig

Braille

milk

green tea

newspaper

tomato juice

shaved ice

glasses

pizza

ring

water

jacket

sheet music

sushi

soup

hamburger

iced tea

80→81

I want something, something to eat.

A hot dog, French fries, pizza and pie.

I want something, something to drink.

Hot tea, iced tea, coffee and milk.

I want something, something to wear.

A heavy coat, a warm sweater, mittens and socks.

  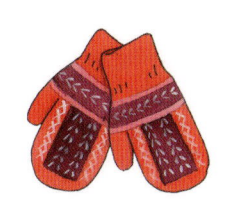 

■ 物や行動の**目的**を言う時は、**to** の後に動作を表す言葉を言います。

何のための **key** かを説明します。

何の目的のために **push** するかを説明します。

a key　to　open　the door

push it　to　open　the door

1 物の目的 （「〜するための」）をはっきりさせる時は **to** + **動作を表す言葉**を使います。

何かほしいなー！ 飲みもの？食べもの？はっきり言って！ 飲みもの？ 食べもの？ 読むもの？

I want something **to** + { **drink** **eat** **read** }.

I have a lot of homework **to** do today.
I need someone **to** help me.
Do you have time **to** help me?

2 行動の目的 （「〜するために」）をはっきりさせる時も **to** + **動作を表す言葉**を使います。

学校に行くのは 何をしに？はっきり言って！ 勉強のため？ 遊ぶため？ 寝るため？

We go to school **to** + { **study** **play** **sleep** }.

One more chant!

82
We go to the bakery to buy some bread.
We go to the library to read some books.
We go to the park to ride a bike.
We go to school to do what?

We are heading for Mars **to** find aliens.

I want | **to go** | to the police box | **to ask** | the way | **to get there.**

〜すること 〜するために 〜するための

3 「〜してうれしい（残念だ）」と言う時も **to** を使います。

I am happy **to** meet you.
I am sorry **to** hear that.

We are very glad to meet you.

Hi!

4 **to ...** を使う決まった表現を練習しましょう。

It's time to go.
It is kind of you to help me.
He was the first man **to** land on the moon.

It's time to go.
Bye!

Let's Write

■ Complete the sentences.

1 I go to school to _____.

2 I go to a supermarket to buy _____.

3 I go to a convenience store to buy _____.

4 I want to go to _____ to _____.

5 I need to buy _____ to _____.

6 We need a ball to play _____ and _____.

Let's Plan and Make a Presentation

Task

To Be Healthy   What do we need to grow and be healthy?
人間が健康に成長するために必要なものを考えて書きましょう。

My Idea

● I need _____ to grow.

● To be healthy, we need _____.

● To have strong muscles, we need _____.

● To fight off colds, we need _____.

Group Summary

● We need _____, _____ and _____ to grow.

● To be healthy, we need _____, _____ and _____.

● To have strong muscles, we need _____, _____ and _____.

● To fight off colds, we need _____, _____ and _____.

Let's Listen

p.72の絵を見ながら答えましょう。

1	2	3	4

Helen Keller

 83

Do you know Helen Keller? Helen Keller was blind and deaf. She could not see or hear.   She was always angry and lonely because she could not communicate with other people. She did not know how to tell her feelings and thoughts to her parents.

One day her parents got a teacher for her. The teacher was a young woman. Her name was Anne Sullivan. She stayed at their house and helped her. Anne taught Helen finger spelling, a type of sign language. She also taught Helen many important things and how to behave herself.

Helen was a very smart and strong girl. She studied very hard. She even learned how to speak. When she was twenty years old, she went to college. She was a very good student at college. She also wrote many books.

(136文字)

84

Smiling is Infectious

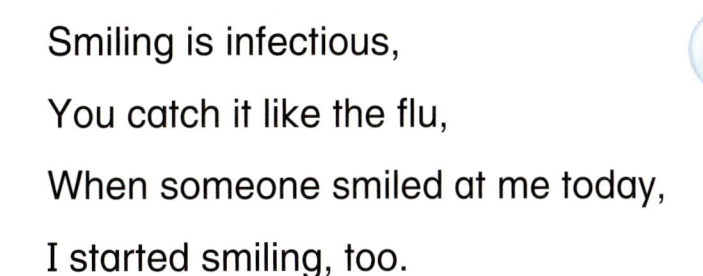

Smiling is infectious,

You catch it like the flu,

When someone smiled at me today,

I started smiling, too.

I walked around the corner,

And someone saw my grin,

When he smiled, I realized,

I'd passed it on to him.

I thought about that smile,

Then I realized its worth.

A single smile, just like mine,

Could travel round the earth.

So, if you feel a smile begin,

Don't leave it undetected.

Let's start an epidemic quick,

And get the world infected.

Learning World BRIDGE ❹ Syllabus

STEP	Topics	Grammar	Let's get started using…	Structures	Words & Phrases	Presentation Theme
1	自分のことを言ってみよう	●be動詞 **Be verbs**	■ I am …. (the characters)	■ I am, you are, we are, they are, he is, she is, it is ■ Am I …? Is he / she …?	I, you, we, they, he, she, it / student, happy, sleepy, great, here, good listener, punctual / be good at, from Japan, in front of	Me & My Friend
2	「これは何？」と言ってみよう	●What+ be動詞 **What+be verbs** ●代名詞の所有格 **Possessives**	■ Is it …? (a rabbit, a cat, a dog/ on, in, behind, in front of/ happy, angry)	■ What is …?　What time …? What day is it …?　What is the date …? ■ your, his, her, our, their, its, Tom's	what, who/ this, that /your, his, her, our, their, its, Tom's / book, bag, eraser, stapler, staple, unidentified object, whale, puppy, sun, star, the earth, capital city	Japanese Items
3	動作を表す言葉を使ってみよう	●一般動詞 命令形 **Imperatives**	■ wash, wash the dishes (25 verbs)	■ Let's … Shall I …? Will you …? Shall we …? Don't …	wash the dishes, give a speech, set the table, eat steak, watch TV, read the newspaper, drive a car, buy groceries, feed the dog, sing a song, open the window, write a letter, drink juice, draw a map, speak French, play soccer, study math, cook curry, practice the piano, ride a bike, close the door, answer the phone, take a picture, bake a cake, make a sandwich	Animals
4	動作を表す言葉を使って自分のことを言ったり質問したりしてみよう	●一般動詞 疑問文と答え方 **Regular verbs**	■ Do you …? (school subjects)	■ Do you like …? Yes, I do. No, I don't.	English, science, Japanese, music, social studies, arts and crafts, PE, math / get up, get on, get off, turn on, turn off, put on, take off, give up, hand in, run away	Cats or Dogs?
5	数をかぞえてみよう	●名詞の単数形／複数形 **Singular/ Plural**	■ How many …? (fruits, vegetables)	■ What are these / those?　They are … ■ How many …?　How much …?	a book-books, a baby-babies, a bus-buses, a knife-knives, a child-children	Let's Make Lunch
6	いろいろなことを質問してみよう	●Wh疑問詞 **Interrogatives**	■ Where, When, How (the museum, the park/ by bike, by car, by bus)	■ What do you want? Where …? When …? Why …? How …? ■ What sport (time / kind of music / grade) …? How old (many / tall / much / often) …?	where, when, how, what, why, who, whose, which / brush your teeth, spell, grandmother, brother, birthday, favorite	Our Favorite Things
7	「物」「人」「事柄」を詳しく言ってみよう	●形容詞 **Adjectives** ●感嘆文 **Exclamatory sentences**	■ Is it …? (little, yellow, purple, orange / a parrot, a goldfish, a squirrel, a rabbit)	■ three beautiful big flowers/ How …! What a …!	duck, turtle / big, small, long, short, round, tiny, large, huge, good, bad, young, old, strong, weak, clean, dirty, shiny, hungry, thirsty, healthy, sweet, difficult, easy, correct, wrong, free, noisy, brave, gentle, lovely, smart, strict, polite, shy, wise, redder, exciting, boring, wonderful, useful, comfortable, dangerous, delicious, necessary	My Opinions
8	できること、できないことを言ってみよう	●助動詞 can **Auxiliary verbs**	■ Can you …? (cook meals, take care of the elderly, clean up the rubble, carry heavy things, do sign language	■ I can …. I can't ….　Can you …? Can I …?　May I …? Could you …?	reach, almost / whistle, ride a unicycle, use an abacus, play the recorder, wink, moonwalk, read music	Our Robot
9	今していることを言ってみよう	●現在進行形 **Present progressive tense**	■ I am …ing. (eat, drink, carry, read, sit, sleep, stand, talk, wear	■ I am …ing.　Are you …ing? No, I am not.　I'm not …ing.	glasses, striped shirt/dancing, washing, crying, thinking, driving, smiling, coming, running, hopping, swimming, chatting, studying, leaving, writing, having, ringing	The Best Excuses

No.	Can-do	文法項目 / Grammar	例題 / Prompt	表現 / Sentence patterns	語彙・表現 / Vocabulary	トピック / Topic
10	第三者のことを話題にしてみよう	●動詞の三人称単数現在 Third-person singular	Lisa's house has … (pointed roof, flat roof, no chimney, two windows, brown door, yellow door)	■ He lives … Does he …? ■ Yes, he does. No, he doesn't. He doesn't … ■ What (Where / When / How / Why) does …? Who …?	does, relax, hungry/runs, comes, reads, walks, helps, speaks, wants, writes, eats, uses, loses, chooses, studies, flies, cries, washes, teaches, goes, has, does, says, lives, drives, starts	Famous People
11	場所を明確に言ってみよう	●前置詞 (場所, 時, 期間, 手段, 方向) Prepositions	There is … There are … (between, in front of, in, on)	■ There is a … in my town. / There are … in a day.	squirrel, annoying, hang around, get off / on, in, under, over, between, by, in front of, behind / at, around, for, before, after, until, by, to, for, with	My Routine and Future Plans
12	動作をもっと詳しく言ってみよう	●副詞 (時, 場所, 程度, 頻度) Adverbs	Find someone who … early, easily, loudly, very much, every day, always, late, regularly	■ You speak … well. See you soon. I'm here. Study harder.	slowly, tight / happily, loudly, gently, clearly, slowly, softly / well, hard, carefully, early, late, fast / soon, now, ago, abroad, here, there, upstairs, home, very, too, either, so, too, harder, more carefully / never, sometimes, often, usually, always	We are proud of you!
13	「これからのこと」を言ってみよう	●未来形 will / be going to Future tense	What will you do in order to be a good speaker of English?	■ I will … / I will be … ■ What are you going to …?	will go swimming, will eat lunch on the beach, will stay home, will read a book, will go outside, will take a walk / moon, astronaut, scientist, interesting program / tomorrow, next year, soon, this evening, tonight, before supper, this weekend	In Twenty Years
14	比べてみよう	●比較級／最上級 Comparatives/Superlatives	Are you taller than …? (tallest, shorter, shortest)	■ I am …er than … / I am the …est in my class. ■ Which is …er, A or B? I run (the) …est in my class.	bigger, cheaper, nicer, better / older-oldest, happier-happiest, easier-easiest, larger-largest, prettier-prettiest, heavier-heaviest, taller-tallest, worse-worst, more, the most, interesting, difficult, famous, popular / fast-faster-the fastest, well-better-the best	Animals in the World
15	過去の状態, その時していたことを言ってみよう	●be動詞の過去形 Past tense be verbs / 過去進行形 Past progressive tense	What was … doing at … o'clock in the morning? (in the afternoon, in the evening, at night)	■ You were … Were you …? Yes, I was. No, I wasn't. I was not … ■ You were …ing. Were you …ing? I wasn't …ing. What (When / Why) was …ing?	busy, tired, sleepy, absent, sick, rainy, cloudy, fine, yesterday, today, tomorrow, last week, last night, at that time was going down the slide, was still sleeping… / were watching…, were cooking… / was meeting his friends…. was eating at the food court…, was playing video games…, was helping his mother… was taking a shower, was having lunch…. was working…, was chatting…, was listening…	Past, Present and Future
16	過去のことを言ってみよう	●一般動詞の過去形 Past tense	Did you …? (clean your room, make your bed, watch TV, study, eat lunch, go shopping)	■ He went to … Did he …? He didn't … ■ Where did you …? What did you …? How much did you …?	played, opened, cleaned, lived, loved, smiled, studied, cried, tried, walked, washed, watched, wanted, visited, started, stopped, dropped, planned / ran, came, saw, went, did, ate, gave, took, spoke, wrote, drank, chose, had, met, made, sat, found, told, left, won, bought, taught, caught, brought, cut, put, set, read	Historical Figures
17	「～すること」を言ってみよう	●動名詞／to 不定詞 (名詞用法) Gerunds / Infinitives (as nouns)	■ What … like doing? What … want to do? What … looking forward to?	■ We like walking … I want to walk …	cooking, go to Italy, working at…, fishing, go to Canada, catching a king salmon, join a choir, drawing pictures… / using, chatting, speaking, talking, walking, go shopping, seeing, be good at playing…, start raining / decide to…, hope to see…, want to be… It is …for…, want to swim, enjoyed swimming, like swimming, like to swim	My Favorite Things to Do
18	何のためのもの, 何のためにするのかを言ってみよう	●to 不定詞 (形容詞用法／副詞用法) Infinitives (as adjectives and adverbs)	Is it something …? (to read, to eat, to drink, to wear)	■ I want something to … I go to school to … I am glad to … I am sorry to …	freezing, something / earrings, map, noodle soup, coffee, hat, curry, cocoa, sneakers, wig, Braille, milk, green tea, newspaper, tomato juice, shaved ice, glasses, pizza, ring, water, jacket, sheet music, sushi, soup, hamburger, iced tea, supermarket, convenience store, muscles, fight off colds	To Be Healthy

It was nice meeting you. See you!

PROGRESS REPORT

My name is

Animal Talk

1	2	3	4	5	6	7	8	9
10	11	12	13	14	15	16	17	18

Let's Chant!

1	2	3	4	5	6	7	8	9
10	11	12	13	14	15	16	17	18

Mini Tests

1	2	3	4	5	6	7	8	9
10	11	12	13	14	15	16	17	18

☆ Challenge Chart ☆

Date	1	2	3	4	5	6	7	8	9	10	11	12	Total
	☺	☺	☺	☺	☺	☺	☺	☺	☺	☺	☺	☺	
	☺	☺	☺	☺	☺	☺	☺	☺	☺	☺	☺	☺	
	☺	☺	☺	☺	☺	☺	☺	☺	☺	☺	☺	☺	
	☺	☺	☺	☺	☺	☺	☺	☺	☺	☺	☺	☺	
	☺	☺	☺	☺	☺	☺	☺	☺	☺	☺	☺	☺	
	☺	☺	☺	☺	☺	☺	☺	☺	☺	☺	☺	☺	
	☺	☺	☺	☺	☺	☺	☺	☺	☺	☺	☺	☺	
	☺	☺	☺	☺	☺	☺	☺	☺	☺	☺	☺	☺	
	☺	☺	☺	☺	☺	☺	☺	☺	☺	☺	☺	☺	
	☺	☺	☺	☺	☺	☺	☺	☺	☺	☺	☺	☺	
	☺	☺	☺	☺	☺	☺	☺	☺	☺	☺	☺	☺	
	☺	☺	☺	☺	☺	☺	☺	☺	☺	☺	☺	☺	
	☺	☺	☺	☺	☺	☺	☺	☺	☺	☺	☺	☺	
	☺	☺	☺	☺	☺	☺	☺	☺	☺	☺	☺	☺	
	☺	☺	☺	☺	☺	☺	☺	☺	☺	☺	☺	☺	
	☺	☺	☺	☺	☺	☺	☺	☺	☺	☺	☺	☺	
	☺	☺	☺	☺	☺	☺	☺	☺	☺	☺	☺	☺	
	☺	☺	☺	☺	☺	☺	☺	☺	☺	☺	☺	☺	
	☺	☺	☺	☺	☺	☺	☺	☺	☺	☺	☺	☺	
	☺	☺	☺	☺	☺	☺	☺	☺	☺	☺	☺	☺	
	☺	☺	☺	☺	☺	☺	☺	☺	☺	☺	☺	☺	
	☺	☺	☺	☺	☺	☺	☺	☺	☺	☺	☺	☺	

Date	1	2	3	4	5	6	7	8	9	10	11	12	Total
	☺	☺	☺	☺	☺	☺	☺	☺	☺	☺	☺	☺	
	☺	☺	☺	☺	☺	☺	☺	☺	☺	☺	☺	☺	
	☺	☺	☺	☺	☺	☺	☺	☺	☺	☺	☺	☺	
	☺	☺	☺	☺	☺	☺	☺	☺	☺	☺	☺	☺	
	☺	☺	☺	☺	☺	☺	☺	☺	☺	☺	☺	☺	
	☺	☺	☺	☺	☺	☺	☺	☺	☺	☺	☺	☺	
	☺	☺	☺	☺	☺	☺	☺	☺	☺	☺	☺	☺	
	☺	☺	☺	☺	☺	☺	☺	☺	☺	☺	☺	☺	
	☺	☺	☺	☺	☺	☺	☺	☺	☺	☺	☺	☺	
	☺	☺	☺	☺	☺	☺	☺	☺	☺	☺	☺	☺	
	☺	☺	☺	☺	☺	☺	☺	☺	☺	☺	☺	☺	
	☺	☺	☺	☺	☺	☺	☺	☺	☺	☺	☺	☺	
	☺	☺	☺	☺	☺	☺	☺	☺	☺	☺	☺	☺	
	☺	☺	☺	☺	☺	☺	☺	☺	☺	☺	☺	☺	
	☺	☺	☺	☺	☺	☺	☺	☺	☺	☺	☺	☺	
	☺	☺	☺	☺	☺	☺	☺	☺	☺	☺	☺	☺	
	☺	☺	☺	☺	☺	☺	☺	☺	☺	☺	☺	☺	
	☺	☺	☺	☺	☺	☺	☺	☺	☺	☺	☺	☺	
	☺	☺	☺	☺	☺	☺	☺	☺	☺	☺	☺	☺	
	☺	☺	☺	☺	☺	☺	☺	☺	☺	☺	☺	☺	
	☺	☺	☺	☺	☺	☺	☺	☺	☺	☺	☺	☺	
	☺	☺	☺	☺	☺	☺	☺	☺	☺	☺	☺	☺	

先生の質問に答えて色をぬりましょう。　　　　Students color in one happy face at a time on answering each of the teacher's questions during warm up/review time.

Certificate of Achievement

Awarded to _____

this _____ day of _____,

for your great effort in

Learning World BOOK 4 BRIDGE

Signed